First World War

and Army of Occupation

War Diary

France, Belgium and Germany

3 DIVISION
Divisional Troops
57 Field Company Royal Engineers
4 August 1914 - 30 June 1915

WO95/1403/2

The Naval & Military Press Ltd
www.nmarchive.com
Published in association with The National Archives

Published by

The Naval & Military Press Ltd

Unit 10 Ridgewood Industrial Park,

Uckfield, East Sussex,

TN22 5QE England

Tel: +44 (0) 1825 749494

www.naval-military-press.com

www.nmarchive.com

This diary has been reprinted in facsimile from the original. Any imperfections are inevitably reproduced and the quality may fall short of modern type and cartographic standards.

Contents

Document type	Place/Title	Date From	Date To
Heading	WO95/1403/2		
Heading	3rd Division 57th Fld Coy R.E. Aug 1914-Jly 1915		
Heading	R.E. 57th Field Coy. War Diary Aug-Dec 1914		
Heading	121/742 War Diary 57th Field Co. R.G. 3rd Division Vol I 4.8-8.9.14		
War Diary	Belford Camp	04/08/1914	04/08/1914
War Diary	Amesbury	16/08/1914	16/08/1914
War Diary	Roven	19/08/1914	19/08/1914
War Diary	Aulnoye	21/08/1914	21/08/1914
War Diary	Cuesnes	22/08/1914	22/08/1914
War Diary	Frameriess	23/08/1914	23/08/1914
War Diary	Bermeries	24/08/1914	24/08/1914
War Diary	Troisville	25/08/1914	08/09/1914
Heading	121/1230 57th Coy RE 3rd Division Volume II 1-30.9.1914		
War Diary		01/09/1914	30/09/1914
Heading	121/1807 57th Field Coy. R.E 3rd Division Vol III 1-31.10.14		
War Diary		01/10/1914	31/10/1914
Heading	121/2599 57th Field Coy: R.E Vol IV 1-30.11.14		
War Diary		01/11/1914	30/11/1914
Heading	121/3889 57th Field Coy. RE Vol V 1-31.12.14		
War Diary	Westoutre	01/12/1914	31/12/1914
Heading	3rd Div R.E 57th Field Coy, War Diary, Jan-July, 1915		
Heading	121/4195 3rd Division 57th Coy. R.E Vol VI		
War Diary		01/01/1915	31/01/1915
Heading	121/4586 3rd Division 57th Field Coy R.E Vol VII 1-28.2.15		
War Diary		01/02/1915	28/02/1915
Heading	121/4939 3rd Division 57th Coy RE Vol VIII 1-31.3.15		
War Diary		01/03/1915	31/03/1915
Heading	121/5195 3rd Division 57th Coy R.E Vol IX 1-30.4.15		
War Diary		01/04/1915	30/04/1915
Heading	121/5610 46th Division 57th Coy R.E Vol X 1-31.5.15		
War Diary		01/05/1915	31/05/1915
Heading	121/5885 2nd Division 57th Coy: R.E Vol XI 1-30.6.15		
War Diary		01/06/1915	30/06/1915
War Diary		01/06/1915	25/06/1915
Heading	49th Div. War Diary of 54th Field Coy. R.E Period. April To July 1915		
Heading	121/6292 3rd Division 57th Field Coy: R.E Vol XII July 15		
War Diary		01/07/1915	31/07/1915
War Diary		01/07/1915	30/07/1915
War Diary		26/06/1915	30/06/1915
Miscellaneous	Health At Nouvelle		
Miscellaneous	Sept 1914		

3RD DIVISION

57TH FLD COY R.E.

AUG 1914 - JLY 1915

To 49 DIV AUG 1915

~~Box 1079~~

Index..........................

SUBJECT.

3RD DIV

No.	Contents.	Date.
	R.E.,	
	57TH FIELD COY,	
	WAR DIARY,	
	AUG - DEC, 1914	

(56,425). Wt.24,741—161. 2000. 11/20. Gp.164. A.&E.W.

War Diary 121/742

57th Field Co. R.E. 3rd Division   Secn. G AG. 7. T. M.T. 2

Vol I. 4.8 — 8.9.14

WAR DIARY or INTELLIGENCE SUMMARY
(ERASE HEADING NOT REQUIRED.)

ARMY FORM C.2118

57 Coy. R.E.

Instructions regarding War Diaries and Intelligence Summaries are contained in F.S. Regs. Part II and the Staff Manual respectively.

HOUR DATE	PLACE	SUMMARY of Events and Information	Remarks and References to Appendices
August 1914.			
4th	Bulford Camp.	Received order to mobilize - most of the horses arrived of the 8th - mobilization Complete 14 August.	
16th	Amesbury	Left Amesbury 10.55 am - started embarking Southampton 7. pm - arrived Rouen 2 am 18 August	
		arrived at Rest Camp CHAMPS DE BRUYERE 12.30 (day) 18th.	
19th	Rouen	Left Rouen night of 19th arr AULNOYE 1.33 pm 20th Aug - billetted + did some work on road improvement at AULNOYE 20th.	
21	AULNOYE	Left billets 7.20 am marched to FEIGNIES	
22	CUESNES	marched to CUESNES received orders to strengthen bridge heads - made 2 light trestle bridges + some barbed wire entanglement + did loopholing - on the early morning of 23rd received order to demolish bridges on orders from III Div. Lt Day was killed in attempting to fix his charges. Lt Boutnois demolished 1 draw bridge + reported that L/cpl Jarvis exhibited great coolness in firing charges under hot infantry fire - Company to HARMIGNIES + NOUVELLE entrenched a position at NOUVELLES lost the pontoons at NOUVELLES - arr at FRAMERIES midnight 22nd	
23	FRAMERIES	ordered to 9th Brigade - erected some barricades in the town - lost 12 bicycles as men were cut off by falling houses in the sudden retirement lost many packs for same reason	
24.	BERMERIES	marched to this place - arrived after dark left at dawn 25. with 9th Brigade.	
		arrived at TROISVILLE evening of 24th Aug - found trenches already commenced.	
25.	TROISVILLE.	The company assisted 9th Brigade to prepare position very little time available before shelling commenced - principle work clearance of foreground by Capt Henderson. Lt Boutnois helped by making some overhead cover + was thus caught in the trenches + lost from his section that day during this action Capt Henderson + Lt Wells with 2 sections were sent via BARTRY to the 7 Brigade at CAUDRY. Lt Parker + his section to AUDENCOURT. Major Howard took No3 Section	

ARMY FORM C. 2118

WAR DIARY or INTELLIGENCE SUMMARY

(ERASE HEADING NOT REQUIRED.)

57 Cy RE

Instructions regarding War Diaries and Intelligence Summaries are contained in F.S. Regs. Part II and the Staff Manual respectively. Title pages will be prepared in manuscript.

Hour, Date, Place	Summary of Events and Information	Remarks and references to Appendices
25.	or rather the mounted portion + half the sappers who were ordered by III Divn to go to BARTRY. The CAUDRY party did not RE-turn. The AUDENCOURT section entrenched a position + eventually retired + joined up with 1 + 4 section at BEAUREVOIR. Major Howard with part of No 3 section + headquarter waggons got into the stream of V Divn + travelling via VERMAND + St SIMON rejoined the rest of the company at HAMS on the 28th. Major Howard prepared the bridge at St SIMON. for demolition + by GOC V Divn orders handed over the firing apparatus to the RE V Divn + went to rejoin III Divn. This he did alone sending the tool carts etc with V Divn	Major Howard joined III Div at HAM
26. + 27th	General retirement via BEAUREVOIR + VERMAND on HAMS	
28.	after marching two successive nights + most of the days. two bridges at HAMS were prepared for demolition. Capt Henderson fired his charges + the demolition was successful. as the German advance was not pressed Lt Boutmois was ordered to withdraw his charges + save his explosives. marched to the S of TARLEFESSE	
29th	To CUTS. picked up head quarter waggons + remainder of company, except pontoons. (Company collected)	

Instructions regarding WAR DIARIES and Intelligence Summaries are contained in F.S. Regs. Part II and the Staff Manual respectively. Title pages will be prepared in manuscript.

WAR DIARY or INTELLIGENCE SUMMARY

(ERASE HEADING NOT REQUIRED.)

57 Coy RE

ARMY FORM C. 2118.

HOUR DATE PLACE	SUMMARY of Events and Information	Remarks and References to Appendices
30 August	Capt Henderson + Lt Wells to BREUGNY at dawn - demolished successfully bridge over the SAMBRO rescued 1 sapper of 59 Coy V Div from some uhlans.	
31 August	moved to MONTOIS	
1 Sept	to VAUCIENNES	
2 Sept	to BOUILLANCY. left at dawn PENCHARD 1 pm. 2nd Sept	
3 Sept	at. PENCHARD	
3 Sept	Left PENCHARD 7.10 am arr MEAUX 8. am 3rd Sept blew up MEAUX bridge (Lt Wells). remainder of Coy destroyed all bridges - weirs. barges + boats between VILLENOYE and TRILPORT - arrived at LA LOGE. ARTUIS. 9. pm. 3 Sept left HAUTE MAISON 10.30 pm 4 Sept. night march to CHATRES	
5 Sept.	arr CHATRES. 7. am	
6 Sept	Left CHATRES 7.30 am arr LUMIGNY 7 pm report that Germans are retiring French pursuing	
7 Sept	left LUMIGNY. 11.30 am - arr LA BRETONNIARE. 8 pm.	
8 Sept	Left LA BRETONNIARE. 5 pm arr LES. FERCHERES. 7 pm	[signature]

121/1230

57th Coy RE.

3rd Division

Volume II. 1-30.9.14

Nothing for M.T. 2

Sen 9 M.T. 2

ARMY FORM C. 2118.

Instructions regarding WAR DIARIES and Intelligence Summaries are contained in F.S. Regs. Part II and the Staff Manual respectively. Title pages will be prepared in manuscript.

September 1914 WAR DIARY ~~or INTELLIGENCE SUMMARY~~

(ERASE HEADING NOT REQUIRED.)

57 Coy RE

HOUR, DATE, PLACE	SUMMARY of Events and Information	Remarks and References to Appendices
September 1st	marched to VAUCIENNES – BOUILLANCY – left at dawn at arrived PENCHARD 1 pm 2nd Sept	
3rd	Left PENCHARD 7 am and arrived at MEUX 8 am – blew up the stone bridge (one span) at MEUX and the foot bridge (3 bays) and partially destroyed the bridge leading over the river to the corn mill destroyed every barge & boat bridge & weir from VILLNOYE to TRILPORT – arrived at LA LOGE ARTUIS 9 pm	
4th	Reconnoitring for positions at LA LOGE ARTUIS	
5th	arrived at CHATRES 2 am	
6th	marched to LUMIGNY – 7th marched to LA BRETONNIARE – 8th marched to LES FERCHERS – 9th crossed the MARNE at NANTEUIL and arrived at VENTELET farm 7 pm – 10th Reached DAMARD 4 pm. II & III Divns came on enemys rear guard near CHEZY. captured 500 prisoners & 6 guns	
11th	Lt Shannon RE joined the company – marched to GRAND ROZOY	
12th	arrived BRENELLE – very wet & stormy – Cavalry action at BRAINE	
13th	Big battle going on at SOISSONS – Engineer reconnaissance of VAILLY valley	

September 1914 WAR DIARY or INTELLIGENCE SUMMARY (ERASE HEADING NOT REQUIRED.) 57 Coy RE

ARMY FORM C. 2118

Instructions regarding War Diaries and Intelligence Summaries are contained in F.S. Regs. Part II and the Staff Manual respectively. Title pages will be prepared in manuscript.

Hour, Date, Place	Summary of Events and Information	Remarks and References to Appendices
September 1914		
14th	During the night of the 13th/14th 56 + 57 Coys built the pontoon bridge at VAILLY – 57 Coy the foot bridge over destroyed railway bridge	
14th	The 5th Cavalry Brigade crossed pontoon bridge into VAILLY and then owing to want of room + shell fire had to retire. heavy shell fire on canal bridge. Company which had been split up at different places. had to retire after the cavalry had crossed. and eventually assembled in the wood near CHASSENY Capt Wright the A/Adjt 1 Sergt + 2 sappers were killed at the bridge and 1 Cpl wounded	
15th	Remained for the day in the wood near chateau worked at night on the approaches for new bridge	
16th	marched to VAILLY. dismounted only with 1 forage cart of cutting tools + a few picks. worked all night helping the infantry	
17. 18 19 20. 21 22	occupied a sand stone quarry near trenches at top of hill above VAILLY. helped the infantry by cutting communications through the woods – entrenching revetting trip wires wire entanglements etc. men suffered principally – from want of sleep + exposure to rain + cold Lt Parker very ill from exposure. only 1 man wounded by stray bullet	

September 1914 — WAR DIARY or INTELLIGENCE SUMMARY (ERASE HEADING NOT REQUIRED.) — 57 Coy RE — ARMY FORM C. 2118

Instructions regarding WAR DIARIES and Intelligence Summaries are contained in F.S. Regs. Part II and the Staff Manual respectively. Title pages will be prepared in manuscript.

HOUR, DATE, PLACE	SUMMARY OF EVENTS AND INFORMATION	Remarks and References to Appendices
23rd Sept	Completed work of entanglement in wood for 16 Brigade. Marched at night to CHASSENEY	
24th + 25 Sept.	Rested at CHASSENEY + checked tools – issued clothing etc. Marched at dusk to BRUNELLE.	
26. 27. 28 – 29	Worked on the position East of BRUNELLE. Long day, work	
30th	Built pontoon bridge over River Aisne in the night. 250 yards up stream of demolished railway bridge. 1 Trestle + 7 pontoons – the approaches required two nights previous work, as banks are steep – Sent 1 section under Lt Boshom to billet at PRESLES, to watch bridge + repair any damage of shell fire	
	30 Sept 14 F J Howard Major RE O.C. 57 Coy RE	

121/1807.

57th Field Coy: R.E

3rd Division.

Vol. III 1—31.10.14.

Instructions regarding WAR DIARIES and Intelligence Summaries are contained in F.S. Regs Part II and the Staff Manual respectively. Title pages will be prepared in manuscript.

WAR DIARY
or
INTELLIGENCE SUMMARY
(ERASE HEADING NOT REQUIRED.)

57th (Field) Coy R.E.

ARMY FORM C. 2118.

October 1914.

HOUR, DATE, PLACE	SUMMARY of Events and Information	Remarks and References to Appendices
1st Oct.	57 Coy billeted at BRUNELLE – worked on the trenches – on the BRUNELLE position	
2nd Oct.	Received orders to go with 9th Brigade to General Reserve – worked in the morning on the ~~the~~ position – marched 7. pm	
3rd Oct	arrived at CRAMAILLE midnight	
	marched 6 pm. and arrived at TROISNES – 2 am 4th Oct	
4th Oct	marched 6.30. pm and arrived CREPY 3 am 5 Oct	
	marched 6.30 pm and arrived RHUIS 1 am 6 Oct	
6 Oct	HQ. & No 2 marched 6 am 6. Oct. and arrived PONT ST MAXENCE 12 noon 6 Oct and entrained	
	No 1 Section marched 3 am and arrived at LE MEUX at 6 am & entrained	
	No 3 Section marched 6.30 and arrived at LONGUEIL at 9 am & entrained	
	The various sections detrained in the vicinity of ABBEVILLE during the morning of the 7 Oct and marched to PONT LE GRAND. arriving there by 6 pm on the 7 Oct	
8. Oct	The company rested at PONT LE GRAND	
9 Oct	Left ~~Foll~~ PONT LE GRAND – 2 am. arrived TOLLENT 8 am	

Instructions regarding WAR DIARIES [illegible]

ARMY FORM C.2118

WAR DIARY or INTELLIGENCE SUMMARY

(ERASE HEADING NOT REQUIRED.)

57 (Field) Coy RE

– October 1914 –

Hour, Date, Place	Summary of Events and Information	Remarks and References to Appendices
October 9th	Left TOLLENT. 5.30 pm marched all night and arrived at TANGRY 10 am 10th oct	
10th oct.	Rested TANGRY	
11 oct	marched from TANGRY 8 am arrived L'ECLEME. 6. pm	
12 oct	marched 7 am arrived LES LOBES 6 pm reported that our force had found right flank of German Army – desultory fighting going on. country very difficult for Artillery + Cavalry – masses of French Cavalry passing our column.	
13 oct	marched 5 am arrived VIELLE CHAPELLE 5. pm. very rainy weather – our force slowly advancing –	
14 oct – 15 oct.	Remained in VIELLE CHAPELLE. made ladder bridges for the infantry to cross dykes. about 80 of these were made	
16 oct.	Marched to RUE DU BOQUETAIRE	
17 oct	Lt Bahsois admitted to hospital	
18 oct	marched to PIETRO	

WAR DIARY or INTELLIGENCE SUMMARY

(ERASE HEADING NOT REQUIRED.)

ARMY FORM C. 2118.

Instructions regarding WAR DIARIES and Intelligence Summaries are contained in F. S. Regs Part II and the Staff Manual respectively. Title pages will be prepared in manuscript.

57 (Field) Coy RE

October 1914

HOUR, DATE, PLACE	SUMMARY of Events and Information	Remarks and References to Appendices
19. 20. 21 Oct	Work on the wire entanglements and trenches on the HERLIES L'IVENTURE line – and also on the second line through LA CLIQUETERIE marched late at night 21 Oct to retired position	
22. 23 24. 25 26	Worked at night on the wire entanglements + head cover of the new position – very difficult to make any progress owing to sniping and the unsettled state of affairs – However a complete entanglement was put all along the front of the 9 Brigade on the 24 the Germans broke through on our left and on the 26 the Germans broke through on our right. men getting very run down from want of sleep and wet – material were got up for head cover. planks + sand bags ~~and~~ and typical shelters made – but the night attacks + fatigued state of infantry prevented the work being carried on except very slowly. The infantry are getting on with the trench work as well as they can	

WAR DIARY OR INTELLIGENCE SUMMARY
(ERASE HEADING NOT REQUIRED.)

ARMY FORM C. 2118.

Instructions regarding WAR DIARIES and Intelligence Summaries are contained in F.S Regs Part II and the Staff Manual respectively. Title pages will be prepared in manuscript.

HOUR, DATE, PLACE	SUMMARY of Events and Information	Remarks and References to Appendices
27. 28. 29.	Ordered to guard the cross roads and defend the village of CROIX BARBEE. Entrenched the company – at night sent sections not required to continue the work of entangling the trenches especially where the right of the 9th Brigade had to be withdrawn owing to 7th Brigade having fallen back	
30th	Ordered to join the LAHORE Division – marched to SAILLY & billetted there –	
31.	Commenced work on the precautionary trenches which are being made in case force has to fall back – clearing foreground – and putting up wire Entanglements	

[illegible]
Major RE
O.C. 57 Coy RE

31st Oct 1914

3rd Division 121/2599

D.F.W. AG7

57th Field Coy: RE.

Vol IV 1—30.11.14

nothing for MI2

57 Coy R. E

Army Form C. 2118.

Instructions regarding War Diaries and Intelligence Summaries are contained in F. S. Regs., Part II. and the Staff Manual respectively. Title pages will be prepared in manuscript.

WAR DIARY
or
~~INTELLIGENCE SUMMARY.~~
(*Erase heading not required.*)

Hour, Date, Place	Summary of Events and Information	Remarks and references to Appendices
November 1914		
1	Worked on the second position in front of SAILLY	
2.	made pontoon bridge + approaches over the River LYS at ESTRAIRE	
3.	Same work as 1st	
4.	Night work on second position at ROUGE CROIX – digging trenches – clearing the ground – making entanglements – demolishing + burning houses.	
5. 6. 7. 8. 9. 10. 11. 12. 13	work on second position trenches – entanglements – + cover for support trenches.	
14.	ordered to move from SAILLY to ESTRAIRE	
15	ordered to move from ESTRAIRE to BAILLEUL	
16.	Rested in BAILLEUL – left the Lahore Division came under I Division	
17.	ordered to march to DRANOUTRE	
18. 19. 20. 21. 22	Night work on the trenches of 1st Brigade I Division – wire entanglement – Cover for support trenches etc	
23.	ordered to march to MONT NOIR + come under III Division	
24. 25. 26	Road making – hutting – charcoal burning – making bombs – making shelters for horses.	

(9 29 6) W2791 100,000 8/14 H W V Forms/C. 2118/11

Army Form C. 2118

WAR DIARY
or
~~INTELLIGENCE SUMMARY.~~
(Erase heading not required.)

57 Coy R.E.

Instructions regarding War Diaries and Intelligence Summaries are contained in F. S. Regs., Part II. and the Staff Manual respectively. Title pages will be prepared in manuscript.

Hour, Date, Place	Summary of Events and Information	Remarks and references to Appendices
27	marched to KEMMEL – night work on trenches before WYTSCHAETE	
28. 29	night work on trenches – improving communications principally –	(Lt Parker wounded) (1 man wounded)
30 –	marched back to MONT NOIR on relief of 9th Brigade	
	J P Howard Major RE O.C. 57 Coy RE 30 Nov 1914	

(9 29 6) W 2794 100,000 8/14 H W V Forms/C. 2118/11

A9/5
D.F.W.

3rd Division

121
3889

57th Field Coy: RE.

Vol V. 1-31.12-14

nil for M.T.2

Instructions regarding War Diaries and Intelligence Summaries are contained in F. S. Regs., Part II. and the Staff Manual respectively. Title pages will be prepared in manuscript.

WAR DIARY
or
~~INTELLIGENCE SUMMARY~~. 57th (Field) Coy. R.E

(Erase heading not required.)

Army Form C. 2118

Hour, Date, Place	Summary of Events and Information	Remarks and references to Appendices
Westoutre 1st 2nd 3rd 4th 5th Dec:	Building huts at Westoutre & Scherpenberg	6k
6th	Marched to Kemmel night work on trenches before Wytschaete	
7 & 8th	night work on trenches, drainage & barbed wiring	
9th	returned to Mont Noir on relief of 9th Brigade	
10th 11th	hutting & stabling at Westoutre	
12th	march to Kemmel	
13. 14. 15.	Work on trenches at WYTECHETE and march back	
16-17 18 . 19 - 20	Work on road - Hutting - Boat gun making - fitting dials to 9th Infy Brigade rifles for firing grenades	
21 22. 23 24.	Marched to KEMMEL. work on two saps. and on four supporting points. on trenches opposite WYTECHETE. - The R.E. field coys carry too few cutting tools such as felling axes - saws. Signalling apparatus is no use. I have found the pumps & hose no use so far in this War. marched to billets morning of 24 Dec	

Instructions regarding War Diaries and Intelligence Summaries are contained in F. S. Regs., Part II. and the Staff Manual respectively. Title pages will be prepared in manuscript.

WAR DIARY or ~~INTELLIGENCE SUMMARY.~~

(*Erase heading not required.*)

57th (Field) Coy R.E.

Army Form C. 2118.

Hour, Date, Place	Summary of Events and Information	Remarks and references to Appendices
25. 26. 27 28. 29 30	Work on corduroying the WESTOUTRE - LOCRE road infantry working party of 50 men daily employed on this work party sent to BAILLEUL (11 sappers) to remain there and work in the shops at bomb gun making - bombs - troughs for the trenches etc Various odd jobs such as bath house for infantry at WESTOUTRE and detachment at various places to instruct infantry of 9th Brigade in making of hurdles - fascines - revetments - wooden & iron loopholes drainage of trenches - hand grenades - rifle grenades - the construction & use of grenades - hutting - furnishing of floors to huts at Scherpenberg - making snow ploughs etc	
31st	marched from Mont Noir to KEMMEL for work on the trenches & supporting points - one section under 2Lt [illegible] proceeded to KEMMEL on afternoon of 30th	

J. S. Howard
Major R.E.
O.C. 57 Coy R.E.

31 Dec 1914

(9 29 6) W 2794 100,000 8/14 H W V Forms/C. 2118/11.

Index..............................

SUBJECT.

3RD DIV.

No.	Contents.	Date.
	R.E.,	
	57TH FIELD COY.,	
	WAR DIARY,	
	JAN - JULY, 1915	
	Transferred to 49 Div 10.8.15	

(56,425). Wt.24,741—161. 2000. 11/20. Gp.164. A.&E.W.

Nil

A97
D7W

3rd Division

121/4195.

57th Coy: R.E.

Vol VI 1-31. 1. 15

Instructions regarding War Diaries and Intelligence Summaries are contained in F. S. Regs., Part II. and the Staff Manual respectively. Title pages will be prepared in manuscript.

WAR DIARY
or
~~INTELLIGENCE~~ SUMMARY.
(Erase heading not required.)

57th Coy R.E

Army Form C. 2118.

Hour, Date, Place	Summary of Events and Information	Remarks and references to Appendices
January 1915		
1st. 2nd. 3rd. 4th.	Work on the trenches and on the supporting points in front of KEMMEL. Working parties of 200 infantry were employed on each of these nights principally carrying up material for the work. 32 carpenters of the 9th Infantry Brigade were collected together & started at work in the Brewery at Kemmel making up trench boxes & chevaux de frise etc.	
4th.	marched to Mont Noir.	
5. 6. 7.	Work on road WESTOUTRE - LOCRE.	
	Work on Hospital. BERTHEN.	
	Training Infantry Pioneers	
8th.	marched to KIMMEL	
9. 10. 11	Work on trenches & supporting points	
12	marched to Mont NOIR	
13. 14. 15	Work on roads. Training infantry Pioneers. Berthen Hospital shed work	
16	marched to KIMMEL. No 4 Section from composite company under Capt Dawson rejoined the 57 Company.	

(9 29 6) W2794 100,000 8/14 H W V Forms/C. 2118/11

Instructions regarding War Diaries and Intelligence Summaries are contained in F. S. Regs., Part II. and the Staff Manual respectively. Title pages will be prepared in manuscript.

WAR DIARY or INTELLIGENCE SUMMARY.

(Erase heading not required.)

57 Coy RE

Army Form C. 2118

Hour, Date, Place	Summary of Events and Information	Remarks and references to Appendices
January 1915		
17. 18. 19	During these nights & the night of the 20 Jan the company worked on the trenches & supporting points – Owing to the darkness and the wet progress was very slow – Incessant work was required to keep the trenches from filling with water – The carpenters of the 9 Infy Brigade are now organised into a regular working party – These 30 men turn out good work for the trenches and the Brewery at Kemmel – The Infantry Pioneers now about 20 per battn are commencing to work for their battalions	
20	marched to Mont Noir – Capt Edwards rejoined	
21. 22. 23	worked on the repair of roads – assisted in the hutting operations at Locre – Continued training of infantry pioneers	
24	Marched to Kemmel.	
24 25 26 27– 28 29 30 31	Worked on the trenches and supporting points during the night. marched to Mont Noir 28th – work on bed for 9.2 Howitzer. Taring huts Westoutre Huts Locre.	

J F Howard Maj RE
O.C. 57 Coy RE

(9 29 6) W2791 100,000 8/14 H W V Forms/C. 2118/11

A.97
D.7W

3rd Division

121
4586

57th Field Coy: RE

Vol XII 1–28.2.15.

Nil

Instructions regarding War Diaries and Intelligence Summaries are contained in F. S. Regs., Part II. and the Staff Manual respectively. Title pages will be prepared in manuscript.

WAR DIARY ~~or~~ ~~INTELLIGENCE SUMMARY.~~

(*Erase heading not required.*)

57 Coy RE

Army Form C. 2118.

Hour, Date, Place	Summary of Events and Information	Remarks and references to Appendices
Feb 1915		
1st	Marched to KEMMEL – employed on the supporting points – laying out & digging a trench in front line – about 150 infantry were employed each night as	
2. 3. 4th	carrying parties taking up sandbags, corrugated iron etc.	
5th	Marched to Mont Noir. employed on small odd jobs – the reinforcements were giving a few hours drill in pontoon & trestle work – No 1 Section was left behind at CLYTEE to commence the barbed wire entanglement	
5. 6. 7. 8	in front of Second line – Inoculation going on steadily.	
9th	Marched to KEMMEL	
9. 10. 11. 12.	During the nights – the company worked on the trenches – & supporting points a few men were employed during the day in charge of infantry parties working on Reserve Line – Some entanglements were put up on the Second line	
13 –	Marched to Mont Noir.	
14. 15. 16.	Employed hutting at Clytte where one Section was billetted – hutting at Locre where 12 men were billetted.	

(9 29 6) W 2791 100,000 8/14 H W V Forms/C. 2118/11.

Instructions regarding War Diaries and Intelligence Summaries are contained in F.S. Regs., Part II. and the Staff Manual respectively. Title pages will be prepared in manuscript.

WAR DIARY ~~or~~ ~~INTELLIGENCE~~ SUMMARY.

(*Erase heading not required.*)

Army Form C. 2118.

57 Coy RE

Hour, Date, Place	Summary of Events and Information (February 1915)	Remarks and references to Appendices
14. 15. 16	(Continued) – Covering Westoutre Huts – making fascines for bed of road of 15" Howitzer – and other odd jobs. 12 men are now semi permanently employed in the shops at Bailleul – making up bomb guns – platforms for machine guns. etc etc	
17.	Marched to Kemmel – the 9th Brigade ordered to YPRES. and the Company ordered to march back to WESTOUTRE.	
18. 19. 20 21	making fascines & laying road & bed for 15" Howitzer – hutting WESTOUTRE Hutting at LOCRE. Various other odd jobs –	
22.	Marched to KEMMEL – on the 21st Capt Dawson left for the 23 Coy & 2nd Lt Hunter arrived in his place –	
22. 23. 24 25	Company worked on the entanglements & clearing of Reserve Line – (NO 11483 Sapper Gadd. C. wounded 23rd) – parties were sent to repair & keep in order the supporting points – & to help in the trenches	
26.	Marched from Kemmel to Mont Noir. one section to La Clytte for work on Second line. & hutting.	
27	Hutting at LOCRE, experiments with Ammonal	

Army Form C. 2118.

Instructions regarding War Diaries and Intelligence Summaries are contained in F. S. Regs., Part II. and the Staff Manual respectively. Title pages will be prepared in manuscript.

WAR DIARY ~~or~~ ~~INTELLIGENCE SUMMARY~~.

(*Erase heading not required.*)

57th Coy R.E.

Hour, Date, Place	Summary of Events and Information	Remarks and references to Appendices
	February 1915	
28th	Parties of pioneers from 85th Bde trained in Field Works. Hutting at LOCRE. Experiments with Trench mortars.	
	C R Edwards Capt RE O.C. 57th Coy R.E. 1.3.15	

(9 29 6) W 2794 100,000 8/14 H W V Forms/C. 2118/11.

3rd Division

181/4939

57th Coy: RE.

Vol VIII 1 – 31.3.15.

Instructions regarding War Diaries and Intelligence Summaries are contained in F. S. Regs., Part II. and the Staff Manual respectively. Title pages will be prepared in manuscript.

WAR DIARY ~~or~~ ~~INTELLIGENCE~~ SUMMARY.

(Erase heading not required.)

57th Coy. R.E.

Army Form C. 2118.

Hour, Date, Place	Summary of Events and Information	Remarks and references to Appendices
	March 1915	
1st 2nd 3rd	Parties of pioneers from 85th Brigade trained in Field Works. Officers of 85th Brigade given instruction in grenade throwing. Hutting at LOCRE. Experiments with Ammonal.	
4th	Marched to KEMMEL, marked out new trenches (No 11151 Sapper Doney E and No 20351 Sapper Palmer E wounded)	
5th	Marked out new trenches (No 33 Corporal Northover G, No 15793 Sapper Pinch A, & No 23365 Pioneer Vinter. C wounded) and superintended digging of new trench.	
6th	Marked out new trenches (No 9479 Sapper Stoddart W wounded).	
7th – 13th	Marked out new trenches, superintended digging of new trenches by infantry, dug new trench & broke out saps. (Casualties:– 7th No 19722 L/Cpl Johnson E wounded; 9th No 28939 Sergt Wyatt W, wounded; 11th No 20137 Sapper Murray J and No 2060 Sapper Peters L wounded; 12th No 23921 Sapper Kay, A., and No 23356 Sapper Regan, H. Killed; No 18590 Sapper Reynolds, F. wounded)	
14th	Marched back to MONT NOIR from KEMMEL	
15th 16th 17th	Hutting at DRANOUTRE. Making fascines.	
17th	Composite company consisting of 1+2 Sections 57 Coy and 1+2 Sections South Midland Field Coy RE. marched to Kemmel	

(9 29 6) W 2791 100,000 8/14 H W V Forms/C. 2118/11.

Instructions regarding War Diaries and Intelligence Summaries are contained in F. S. Regs., Part II. and the Staff Manual respectively. Title pages will be prepared in manuscript.

WAR DIARY
or
INTELLIGENCE SUMMARY.
(Erase heading not required.)

57 Coy RE

Army Form C. 2118.

Hour, Date, Place	March 1915 Summary of Events and Information	Remarks and references to Appendices
18. 19. 20. 21 22.	During these nights the Composite Company as detailed before	
23	worked on the trenches at Kemmel principally making communication trenches from the trenches to the rear	
	No 3 + 4 Sections 57th Coy + 3 + 4 Sections S. Fd Coy RE. worked on bydges howitzer, fascines & hurdles.	
23.	The Composite company returned to Mont Noir	
23	The 57 Coy reconstituted. marched from Mont Noir to DICKEBUSCH & billetted there.	
24.	Company worked on trenches near St ELOI.	
25 26 27 28.	Company worked on trenches near St ELOI. with an average of 400 infantry per night.	
29. 30. 31.	Worked on trenches & defences about St ELOI.	
31	Capt Finnimore transferred to 56 Coy. 2Lt Dyer arrived on 30th	

J P Howard
Major
O.C. 57 Coy

(9 29 6) W 2794 100,000 8/14 H W V Forms/C. 2118/11.

1

3rd Division

121/5195

57th Coy: RE

Vol IX 1–30.4.15

A87
2772

Instructions regarding War Diaries and Intelligence Summaries are contained in F. S. Regs., Part II. and the Staff Manual respectively. Title pages will be prepared in manuscript.

WAR DIARY
or
~~INTELLIGENCE SUMMARY.~~
(Erase heading not required.)

57 Coy R.E.

Army Form C. 2118.

Hour, Date, Place	Summary of Events and Information	Remarks and references to Appendices
April		
1st 2nd 3rd	Work on trenches round St ELOI	
4th	remained DICKEBUSCH	
5th	marched to LOCRE. half Coy went to KEMMEL	
	½ Coy unable to get billets in LOCRE went to Mont Noir	
6.	Sections at Kemmel went to work on trenches – and	
	Sections at Mont Noir marched to LOCRE. Saw the	
	CRE North Midland Division + arranged for Engineer	
	Stores etc	
7.	Work on trenches opposite Kemmel –	
8. 9. 10. 11. 12	half the company worked at Kemmel and half remained in Locre	
13.	No 3 Section under Lieut Joseph was sent to Neuve Eglise to be	
	attached to the 1st North Midland Field Company to help them	
	one section of this Territorial unit joined the 57 Coy for instruction	
14 – 15	No 1 + 2 Sections + Territorial Section worked at Kemmel. No 25173 Spr	
	A Sheet. died of wounds	
16.	No 2066 Spr. Bartlett W. and No 23742 Pr. Topham. T. wounded.	

Instructions regarding War Diaries and Intelligence Summaries are contained in F. S. Regs., Part II. and the Staff Manual respectively. Title pages will be prepared in manuscript.

April.

WAR DIARY
or
~~INTELLIGENCE~~ SUMMARY.
(*Erase heading not required.*)

57 Coy RE

Army Form C. 2118.

Hour, Date, Place	Summary of Events and Information	Remarks and references to Appendices
April.		
17. 18. 19. 20. 21.	Worked on trenches in front of Kemmel.	
22 23. 24. 25. 26. 27.	Worked on trenches in front of Kemmel. and on the communication trench 2000 yards long from Kemmel to the trenches. The North Midland Field Coy section returned to its own company on the 27 and No 3 section returned to the 57 same date.	
28. 29. 30.	Continued work on trenches. The communication trench from Kemmel to G4 is now nearly finished 2500 yds long. with wooden foot boards throughout. & drained. the front trenches of the Notts & Derby Brigade are practically complete & wired. & what is still required is efficient sniping loopholes. Lowering of parapets & trenches. & raising of traverses.	
	[signature] Major RE 1 May 1915. O.C. 57 Coy RE	

(9 29 6) W 2794 100,000 8/14 H W V Forms/C. 2118/11

121/5610

46th Division

57th Coy: R. E.

Vol X 1 — 31.5.15

Instructions regarding War Diaries and Intelligence Summaries are contained in F. S. Regs., Part II. and the Staff Manual respectively. Title pages will be prepared in manuscript.

WAR DIARY
or
INTELLIGENCE SUMMARY.
(Erase heading not required.)

May 1915
57 Coy RE

Army Form C. 2118.

Hour, Date, Place	Summary of Events and Information	Remarks and references to Appendices
May 7th	12 O.R. Searchlight section + 10 O.R. Reinforcements joined.	
May 1.2.3.4.5.6.7.8	Worked on trenches in front of Kemmel.	
9.	Took over temporarily the 8th Brigade line in addition to our own. The line is very bad. Communications indifferent + badly drained trenches not joined up. traverses inefficient + never higher than the parapet. no parados. dead still unburied. unsanitary condition generally.	
10	Blew up the mine at C[illegible].	
10	Work on G.H.Q. line laying out + digging support trenches	
	Up to date the following NCOs + men of this Company have received the D.C.M.	
	No 3948 Sergeant. E. G Taylor	
	No 3959. Sapper. W. Winchester	
	No 9946 acting Corporal. J. H. D. Williams	
	No 23921. Sapper. A. Kay	
	No 14692 Sapper T. Rea	
	No 3976 Corporal. C. Jarvis received the Victoria Cross.	

(9 29 6) W2794 100,000 8/14 H W V Forms/C. 2118/11

Instructions regarding War Diaries and Intelligence Summaries are contained in F. S. Regs., Part II. and the Staff Manual respectively. Title pages will be prepared in manuscript.

WAR DIARY
or
INTELLIGENCE SUMMARY.
(Erase heading not required.)

May 1915
57 Coy RE

Army Form C. 2118.

Hour, Date, Place	Summary of Events and Information	Remarks and references to Appendices
May		
11. 12. 13. 14. 15. 16. 17. 18. 19, 20, 21, 22, 23, 24, 25	Worked on S.P.4 * Via Cellia + The Fosse –	
May 19th	Cpl Trump + Sap Worsdell transferred to 177th Tunnelling Coy –	
20th	Wagon L.S. with 2 searchlights arrived –	
24th	Company took over mining in 139th Bde area with an infantry personnel of 2 officers + 36 OR –	
25. 26. 27. 28. 29	– Company worked on the trenches	
30. 31.	Company took over work on the GHQ 2 line in front of Kemmel. and laid out the support trenches. Communications. splinter proofs. for the infantry to dig – While dealing with this line the urgent necessity of extending the defences in front of Kemmel itself becomes apparent. The 139 Infantry Brigade are commencing to move to the left and it is evident that we will have to take over the trenches further north. The mining section is no good at present.	

[illegible] Howard
Major RE
OC 57 Coy RE

(9 29 6) W 2794 100,000 8/14 H W V Forms/C. 2118/11

Instructions regarding War Diaries and Intelligence Summaries are contained in F. S. Regs., Part II. and the Staff Manual respectively. Title pages will be prepared in manuscript.

WAR DIARY
or
~~INTELLIGENCE SUMMARY.~~
(Erase heading not required.)

57 Coy R.E.

Army Form C. 2118.

113

Hour, Date, Place	Summary of Events and Information	Remarks and references to Appendices
	Work on trenches round St ELOI	
	Remained DICKEBUSCH	
	marched to LOCRE. half Coy went to KEMMEL	
	½ Coy unable to get billets in LOCRE went to Mont Noir	
	sections at Kemmel sent to work on trenches and	
	sections at Mont Noir marched to LOCRE. Saw the	
	CRE North Midland Division & arranged for Engineer	
	Stores etc	
	Work on trenches opposite Kemmel.	
	half the company worked at Kemmel and half remained in Locre	
	No 3 Section under Lieut Joseph was sent to Neuve Eglise to be	
	attached to the 1st North Midland Field Company to help them	
	one section of the Territorial unit joined the 57 Coy for instruction	
	No 1 & 2 Sections & Territorial Section worked at Kemmel No 25173 Spr	
	R. Scott [?] died of wounds	
	No 2065 [?] Spr Bartlett W and No 23742 Spr Tipham [?] T. wounded.	

Instructions regarding War Diaries and Intelligence Summaries are contained in F. S. Regs., Part II. and the Staff Manual respectively. Title pages will be prepared in manuscript.

WAR DIARY
or
~~INTELLIGENCE SUMMARY.~~
(Erase heading not required.)

Army Form C. 2118.

57 RE

112

Hour, Date, Place	Summary of Events and Information	Remarks and references to Appendices
April		
19 20 21	Worked on trenches in front of Kemmel	
[illegible] 25 26 27	Worked on trenches in front of Kemmel and on the communication trench 2000 yards long from Kemmel to the trenches. The North Midland Field Coy section returned to its own company on the 27 and No 3 section returned to the 57 same date.	
28 29 30	Continued work on trenches. The communication trench from Kemmel to Coy is now nearly finished 2500 yds long with [illegible] [illegible] [illegible] [illegible] [illegible] of the [illegible] Brigade are practically complete [illegible] still [illegible] [illegible] training [illegible] [illegible] [illegible]	
	[illegible] Major RE	
	1 May 1915 OC 57 Coy RE	

May 1915

57 Coy RE

Army Form C. 2118.

49

2

Instructions regarding War Diaries and Intelligence Summaries are contained in F. S. Regs., Part II. and the Staff Manual respectively. Title pages will be prepared in manuscript.

WAR DIARY
or
INTELLIGENCE SUMMARY.
(Erase heading not required.)

Hour, Date, Place	Summary of Events and Information	Remarks and references to Appendices
May 7th	~~12 O.R. ... Reinforcements joined.~~	
1.2.3.4.5.6.7.8	Worked on trenches in front of Kemmel.	
9.	Took over temporarily the 8th Brigade line in addition to our own. The line is very bad. Communications indifferent & badly drained. trenches not paved up. traverses inefficient & never higher than the parapet. no parados. dead still unburied. Unsanitary conditions generally.	
~~10~~	Blew up the mine at G1.	
10	Work on G.H.Q. line laying out & digging support trenches	
	Up to date the following NCOs & men of this Company have received the D.C.M.	
	No 3948 Sergeant E. G. Taylor	
	No 3959 Sapper W. Winchester	
	No 9946 acting Corporal J. H. D. Williams	
	No 23921 Sapper A. Kay	
	No 14692 Sapper T. Rea	
	No 3976 ~~Sapper~~ C. Jarvis. received the Victoria Cross	

W 2794 100,000 8/14 H W V Forms/C. 2118/11

Instructions regarding War Diaries and Intelligence Summaries are contained in F. S. Regs., Part II. and the Staff Manual respectively. Title pages will be prepared in manuscript.

WAR DIARY
or
INTELLIGENCE SUMMARY.
(Erase heading not required.)

May 1915 — 5/H 57 Coy RE

Army Form C. 2118.

230

Hour, Date, Place	Summary of Events and Information	Remarks and references to Appendices
May 11. 12. 13. 14. 15. 16. 17. 18. [illegible] 22. 23. 24.	Worked on S.P. 4 & [illegible] + the Fosse.	
May 19th	Capt Tromp + Lieut W[illegible] transferred to 177th Tunnelling Coy.	
20th	[illegible] 2 searchlights arrived.	
24th	Company took over mining in 139th Bde area with an infantry personnel of 2 officers + 36 OR.	
25. 27. 28. 29.	Company worked on the trenches.	
30. 31	Company took over work in the C.A.R.2 line in front of Kemmel and [illegible] at the support trenches. Communications, splinter proofs, further infantry [illegible]. While dealing with this line the urgent necessity of extending the defences in front of Kemmel itself became apparent. The 139 Infantry Brigade were commencing to move to the left and it is evident that we will have to take over the trenches further north. The mining section is no good at present.	

H. Hamand
[illegible]

Instructions regarding War Diaries and Intelligence Summaries are contained in F. S. Regs., Part II, and the Staff Manual respectively. Title pages will be prepared in manuscript.

WAR DIARY
or
INTELLIGENCE SUMMARY.
(Erase heading not required.)

May 1915

57 Coy RE

110

Army Form C. 2118.

231

Hour, Date, Place	Summary of Events and Information	Remarks and references to Appendices
May 7th	+2 OR searchlight section + 10 OR Reinforcements joined.	
1.2.3.4.5.6.7.8	Worked on trenches in front of Kemmel.	
9.	Took over temporarily the 8th Brigade line in addition to our own. The line is very bad. Communications indifferent & badly drained. Trenches not joined up. Traverses inefficient & never higher than the parapet. No parados. Dead still unburied. Unsanitary condition generally.	
	Blew up the mine at G1.	
10	Work on GHQ line. Laying out & digging support trenches	
	Up to date the following NCOs & men of this Company have received the D.C.M.	
	No 3948 Sergeant E. G. Taylor	
	No 3959 Sapper W. Winchester	
	No 9946 acting Corporal J. H. D. Williams	
	No 23921 Sapper A. Kay	
	No 14692 Sapper T. Rea	
	No 3976 ~~Sapper~~ Corporal. C. Jarvis received the Victoria Cross	

(9 29 6) W 2794 100,000 8/14 H W V Forms/C. 2118/11.

Instructions regarding War Diaries and Intelligence Summaries are contained in F.S. Regs., Part II. and the Staff Manual respectively. Title pages will be prepared in manuscript.

WAR DIARY
or
INTELLIGENCE SUMMARY.
(Erase heading not required.)

May 1915

5/1/H. 57 Cy RE

(1)

Army Form C. 2118.

230

Hour, Date, Place	Summary of Events and Information	Remarks and references to Appendices
May		
11. 12. 13. 14. 15. 16. 17. 18. 19. 20. 21. 22. 23. 24 incl	Worked on S.P. 4 + via Callin + the Fosse –	
May 19th	Cpt Trump + Lieut Windell transferred to 177th Tunnelling Coy –	
20th	Wagon L.S. + H. 2 Sandbag [illegible] arrived –	
24th	Company took over mining in 139th Bde area with an infantry personnel of 2 officers + 36 O.R.	
25. 26. 27. 28. 29	Company worked on the trenches	
30. 31	Company took over work on the CAHQ line in front of Kennel and land at the support trenches communications – splendid progress for the infantry to dig – While dealing with this line the urgent necessity of extending the defences in front of Kennel itself becomes apparent. The 139 Infantry Brigade are commencing to move to the left and it is evident that we will have to take over the trenches further north. The mining [illegible] is no good at present.	
		H. J. Humand, Major RE, O.C. 57 Coy R.E.

(9 29 6) W 2794 100,000 8/14 H W V Forms/C. 2118/11

24th Division

121/5885

57th Coy: R E

Vol XI 1 — 30. 6. 15.

Instructions regarding War Diaries and Intelligence Summaries are contained in F. S. Regs., Part II. and the Staff Manual respectively. Title pages will be prepared in manuscript.

WAR DIARY
or
INTELLIGENCE SUMMARY.
(Erase heading not required.)

57 Coy RE. Army Form C. 2118.

June 1915

Hour, Date, Place	Summary of Events and Information	Remarks and references to Appendices
1st	The 6th DCLI + 6th Somerset L.I. were employed on night digging during the first relief on the G.H.Q. 2nd Line round Kemmel Hill	
2. 3. 4 5.	The 6th DCLI worked on the subsidiary line – the R.E. put the farms on this line in a state of defence. making bomb proofs in the cellars + putting machine gun emplacements in the corners of houses at ground level	
6 7 8. 9. 10.	The 6. Somerset L.I. furnished the working parties for the subsidiary line – Capt Edwards took over the construction of the New Supporting point VI. and as we were short of RE had to employ the search light detachment for this purpose The following have been awarded the DCM No 28939 Sergt Wyatt No 14337 Sappr. McLaren No 7659 Sappr Meopham	
11. 12. 13. 14. 15. 16. 17	The company worked on defended farms in the subsidiary line + on wire entanglements on this line. Divisional cyclists worked on Subsidiary line in GOETHALS WOOD	

(9 29 6) W 2794 100,000 8/11 H W V Forms/C. 2118/11.

Instructions regarding War Diaries and Intelligence Summaries are contained in F. S. Regs., Part II. and the Staff Manual respectively. Title pages will be prepared in manuscript.

WAR DIARY *or* INTELLIGENCE SUMMARY.

(Erase heading not required.)

57th Coy R.E.

Army Form C. 2118.

June 1915.

Hour, Date, Place	Summary of Events and Information	Remarks and references to Appendices
11. 12. 13. 14. 15. 16. 17	Infantry parties under RE supervision continued work on new S.P.6, infantry carpenters working on revetment.	
	Instruction in running of searchlights was given to detachments from 1st & 2nd North Midland Field Coys RE.	
	No 14692 S.p T. Rea wounded 16th.	
18th	Company worked on defended farms & wire entanglements on subsidiary line.	
	Infantry party under RE supervision worked on new S.P.6.	
19th	Company worked on defended farms in subsidiary line in morning, & infantry party under RE supervision on new S.P.6. Company ~~[illegible]~~ assembled at LOCRE in the evening	
20th	Company marched at 9pm with 139th Brigade to billet 1½ miles S of VLAMERTINGHE ~~[illegible]~~ (H22a 2.6) arriving 1am 21st	
21st	Company moved to billet 300 yards west of previous one. Officers reconnoitred front line.	
22nd, 23	Officers reconnoitred communications, 2nd & 1st lines. Men cleaned up billets & surrounding area	
24	Morning, Company erected cooking shelters & shelters for explosives & constructed water trough. Evening, two sections worked on shelters near ZILLEBEKE ETANG.	
25th	Two sections worked on ~~[illegible]~~ shelters near ZILLEBEKE ETANG.	

Instructions regarding War Diaries and Intelligence Summaries are contained in F. S. Regs., Part II. and the Staff Manual respectively. Title pages will be prepared in manuscript.

WAR DIARY
or
INTELLIGENCE SUMMARY.
(Erase heading not required.)

57th Coy RE — Army Form C. 2118.

June 1915.

Hour, Date, Place	Summary of Events and Information	Remarks and references to Appendices
26th	Two sections worked on defence of ZILLEBEKE	
27	Two sections worked on the defence of Zillebeke. Capt. C. M. Edwards transferred to III Div	
28	Two sections worked on the defence of Zillebeke and	
	the trenches in front of the village. Lt R A Turner joined	
29	Work of Zillebeke village. Lt Turner slightly wounded.	
30	Work on Zillebeke village & road to KRUISTRAAT	

1 July 15

J. P. Howard
Maj RE
O.C. 57 Coy RE

(9 29 6) W 2794 100,000 8/14 H W V Forms/C. 2118/11

Instructions regarding War Diaries and Intelligence Summaries are contained in F.S. Regs., Part II. and the Staff Manual respectively. Title pages will be prepared in manuscript.

Army Form C. 2118.

WAR DIARY or INTELLIGENCE SUMMARY.

(Erase heading not required.)

57 Coy RE

June 1915

109

Hour, Date, Place	Summary of Events and Information	Remarks and references to Appendices
1st	The 6th D.C.L.I. + 6th Somerset L.I. were employed on night digging during the first week on the G.H.Q. 2 line round Kemmel Hill	
2. 3. 4. 5	The 6th DCLI worked on the Subsidiary line – the R.E. put the farms on this line in state of defence – making bomb proofs in the cellars + putting machine gun emplacements in the corners of houses + at ground level	
6. 7. 8. 9. 10	The 6 Somerset L.I. furnished the working parties for the Subsidiary line – Capt Edwards took over the construction of the New Supporting point VI. and as we were short of RE had to employ the search light detachment for this purpose The following have been awarded the DCM No 28739 Sgt. Wyatt No 14337 Sapr. McLaren No 7659 Sapr. Morphew	
11. 12. 13. 14. 15. 16. 17	The company worked on defended farms in the Subsidiary line + on loose entanglements on this line & Divisional Cyclists worked on Subsidiary line in GOETHALS WOOD	

(9 29 6) W 2791 100,000 8/14 H W V Forms/C. 2118/11.

Instructions regarding War Diaries and Intelligence Summaries are contained in F. S. Regs., Part II. and the Staff Manual respectively. Title pages will be prepared in manuscript.

WAR DIARY
or
INTELLIGENCE SUMMARY.
(Erase heading not required.)

57th Coy RE — Army Form C. 2118.

108 — June 1915.

Hour, Date, Place	Summary of Events and Information	Remarks and references to Appendices
11.12.13.14.15.16.17	Infantry parties under RE supervision continued work on new S.P.6, infantry carpenters working on revetment. Instruction in running of searchlights was given to detachments from 1st & 2nd North Midland Field Coys RE. No 14692 Sap T. Rea wounded 16th.	
18th	Company worked on defended farms & entanglements in subsidiary line. Infantry party under RE supervision worked on new S.P.6	
19th	Company worked on defended farms in subsidiary line in morning, & infantry party under RE supervision on new SP 6. Company assembled at LOCRE in the evening	
20th	Company marched at 9pm with 139th Brigade to billet 1½ miles S of VLAMERTINGHE (H22a 2.6) arriving 1am. 21st	
21st	Company moved to billets 300 yards west of previous one. Officers reconnoitred front line.	
22nd 23rd	Officers reconnoitred communications, 2nd & 1st line. Men cleaned up billets & surrounding area	
24	Morning. Company erected cooking shelter & shelter for explosives & constructed latrine trough. Evening two sections worked on shelter near ZILLEBEKE ETANG	
25	Two sections worked on the shelter near ZILLEBEKE ETANG	

(0419) Wt. W3906/P1607 2,500,000 7/15 McA & W Ltd (E 3848) Forms W3091/

Army Form W.3091

Cover for Documents.

Nature of Documents.

War Diary

of

57th Field Coy. R.E.

[illegible]

49th Div.

Notes, or Letters written.

3rd Division

131/6292

57th Field Coy: RE

Vol XII

July 15

Nil

Instructions regarding War Diaries and Intelligence Summaries are contained in F. S. Regs., Part II. and the Staff Manual respectively. Title pages will be prepared in manuscript.

WAR DIARY
or
INTELLIGENCE SUMMARY.
(Erase heading not required.)

July 1915
54th Coy. R.E.

Army Form C. 2118.

Hour, Date, Place	Summary of Events and Information	Remarks and references to Appendices
1. 2. 3. 4. 5.	Half the company worked on the defences of Zillebeke – on 1.2.3 half company worked on road from H_{21} to Kruistraat making a diversion to keep traffic off the pavé road – The work is not getting on very rapidly because (i) it is difficult to get any work done in the day at Zillebeke on account of constant shelling, including shells with asphyxiating gas. (ii) the shortness of the nights (iii) the long distance to the work	
6. 7. 8. 9.	Company still working on the defences of ZILLEBEKE – and other small services in addition.	
10.	Company marched from H_{21} – 46 Divn. V Corps – to near ELVERDINGE 49 Divn. VI Corps. for work on left of line of British Army. on trenches recently captured from Germans	
11	Lt Hunter's section went up to live in trenches – & to open up communications with front trenches	
12. 13.	1 section work on trenches. 3 sections hutting & making brushes – on the 13th night no work could be done on account of German gas attack & shelling	

(9 29 6) W 2794 100,000 8/14 H W V Forms/C. 2118/11.

4 15 16

Instructions regarding War Diaries and Intelligence Summaries are contained in F. S. Regs., Part II. and the Staff Manual respectively. Title pages will be prepared in manuscript.

WAR DIARY
or
INTELLIGENCE SUMMARY.
(Erase heading not required.)

57 Coy R.E. July

Army Form C. 2118.

Hour, Date, Place	Summary of Events and Information	Remarks and references to Appendices
14.	practically no work done on account of pouring rain + darkness – impossible to work during daylight – 15th good work done considering circumstances.	
16.	practically no work done on account of pouring rain + darkness – men all soaked to skin + trenches flooded – It practically amounts to very little progress having been made for six days. Owing (i) To taking over a new line during the counter attacks of Germans (ii) Incomplete knowledge of the line + of what was required to be done (iii) Heavy shelling during the day (iv) Rain + no moon at night – After careful reconnaissance by the R.E. officers of company – a definite scheme of work + requirements was drawn up and on the 16 July explained to the Brigadier + second in command of the batt^ns of the 148 Brigade – So that work in front line should be taken up in proper order + some continuity of effort attained —	
17	Lt Dyer who went sick on 13th sent to Boulogne. 2 Cpl HAWKEN – wounded –	
18. 19 –	Work on trenches + communication trenches 23270 Sapper Gledhill wounded. Supply of timber for all work very inadequate	
20. 21. 22	Work continued on trenches – night of 22/23 Lt Turner commenced putting wire entanglement across canal	

(9 29 6) W 2794 100,000 8/14 H W V Forms/C. 2118/11.

Instructions regarding War Diaries and Intelligence Summaries are contained in F. S. Regs., Part II. and the Staff Manual respectively. Title pages will be prepared in manuscript.

WAR DIARY
or
INTELLIGENCE SUMMARY.
(Erase heading not required.)

July 1915 —

Army Form C. 2118.

54th Coy. R.E.

Hour, Date, Place	Summary of Events and Information	Remarks and references to Appendices
23	night of 23/24 Lt Turner putting up barbed wire entanglement between the French & our lines along canal bank. L/Cpl. Wildgoose killed – No 3 Section shelled Sapper Mackay wounded – decided to bring the section further back as Germans had evidently got the range of their trench –	
24	Work on Canal banks as before. In the evening a reinforcement of 10 arrived, including Sergt Wyatt, who now ranks junior to C.S.M Henwood.	
25.	Major Howard reconnoitres trench railway, Work of footboarding communication trenches is started.	
26	Trench railway laid out.	
27.	Work still being done on communication trenches BARNSLEY ROAD and Canal Bank under R.E. Supervision. Canal bank trench is always "crumped" and so work has to be done again. Footboards were put down by Lt Hunter	

(9 29 6) W 2794 100,000 8/14 H W V Forms/C. 2118/11

Instructions regarding War Diaries and Intelligence Summaries are contained in F. S. Regs., Part II. and the Staff Manual respectively. Title pages will be prepared in manuscript.

WAR DIARY
or
INTELLIGENCE SUMMARY.
(Erase heading not required.)

Army Form C. 2118.

54th (Fd) Coy. R.E.

July 1915.

Hour, Date, Place	Summary of Events and Information	Remarks and references to Appendices
28.	No 17652 Sapper Flint and 24638 Pioneer Rees slightly wounded by shell fire near 63 going to erect notice boards. Sergt Martin was wounded on night work in Westbeck Trench.	
29. 30.	Lt Hunter's section relieved Lt MacLean on night 29/30. Received wire saying Lt Dyer had to be struck off strength on 28th as he had crossed the channel. An N.C.O is being provided by Lt Hunter to supervise traverses in 2nd line being increased to 9' by 5'	
31	Sap Gadd was wounded unloading timber (corduroy bridge). The infantry never turned up to carry.	
*	Lt MacLean started the timber railway bridge.	
	1-8-15	[signature] OC 54th (Fd) Coy R.E.

Instructions regarding War Diaries and Intelligence Summaries are contained in F.S. Regs., Part II. and the Staff Manual respectively. Title pages will be prepared in manuscript.

WAR DIARY
or
INTELLIGENCE SUMMARY.

(Erase heading not required.)

July 1915
54th Corp. R.E.

Army Form C. 2118.

103

Hour, Date, Place	Summary of Events and Information	Remarks and references to Appendices
1. 2. 3. 4. 5	Half the company continued on the defences of Zillebeke; the other half company worked on road from H_{2} to Kruistraat making a diversion to keep traffic off the pavé road. The work is not getting on very rapidly because (i) the difficulty of getting any work done in the day at Zillebeke on account of constant shelling, including shells with asphyxiating gas (ii) the shortness of the nights (iii) the long distance to the work.	
6. 7. 8. 9.	Company still working on the defences of ZILLEBEKE – and the [illegible] [illegible] in rotation.	
10	Company marched from H_{21} – 46 Div – 2 Corps – to near ELVERDINGE 49 Div VI Corps for work on left of line, often [illegible] on trenches recently captured from Germans.	
11	Lt Hunter [illegible] [illegible] [illegible] [illegible] [illegible] [illegible] [illegible]	
12. 13.	[illegible]	

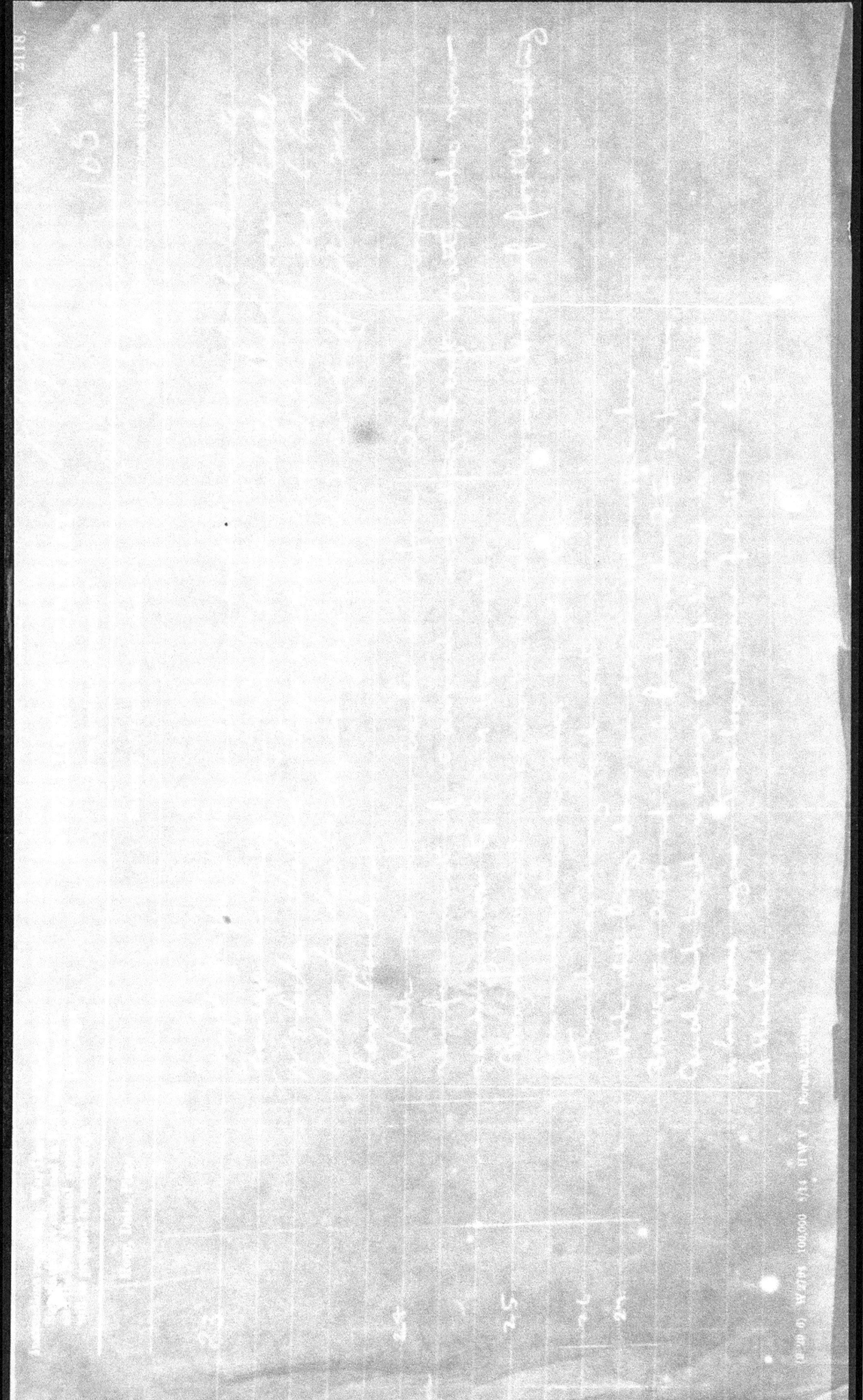

Army Form C. 2118.

Hour, Date, Place		Remarks and references to Appendices
23		
24		
25		
26		
27		

W 2794 100,000 5/14 H W V Forms/C. 2118/11

Instructions regarding War Diaries and Intelligence Summaries are contained in F. S. Regs., Part II. and the Staff Manual respectively. Title pages will be prepared in manuscript.

WAR DIARY
or
INTELLIGENCE SUMMARY.
(Erase heading not required.)

Army Form C. 2118.

54th Fd. Coy. RE.

July 1915.

Hour, Date, Place	Summary of Events and Information	Remarks and references to Appendices
28.	No. 17652 Sapper Flint and 24830 Pioneer Rees slightly wounded by shell fire ... going to erect notice boards. Sergt Martin was wounded on night work in West[illegible] Trench.	
29–30	Lt Hunter's section relieved LT MacLean on night 29/30. Received wire saying Lt Dyson had to be struck off strength on 28th as he had crossed the channel. An NCO [illegible] by Lt Hunter to reinforce traverses in 2nd line being increased to 9' by 5'.	
31	[illegible] Gadd was wounded unloading tubes (cordury bridge) the infantry never turned up to carry.	
	~~Lt MacLean started the cordury bridge.~~	

…ions regarding War Diaries and Intelligence Summaries are contained in F. S. Regs., Part II. …the Staff Manual respectively. Title pages …be prepared in manuscript.

WAR DIARY
or
INTELLIGENCE SUMMARY.

(Erase heading not required.)

57th Coy RE — Army Form C. 2118.

107 — June 1915

Hour, Date, Place	Summary of Events and Information	Remarks and references to Appendices
26th	Two sections worked on defences of ZILLEBEKE	
27	Two sections worked on the defences of Zillebeke. Capt C M Edwards transferred to III [illegible]	
28	Two sections worked on the defences of Zillebeke and the trenches in front of the village. 1st RA Tunnel [illegible]	
29	work of Zillebeke village. [illegible]	
30	work on Zillebeke village + road to KRUISTRAAT [illegible]	
	[illegible] Major RE O.C. 57 Coy RE 1 July 15	
	The following [illegible]	
	[illegible] ZILLEBEKE [illegible]	

W. 1991. 100,000 8/14 H.W.V. Forms/C. 2118/11.

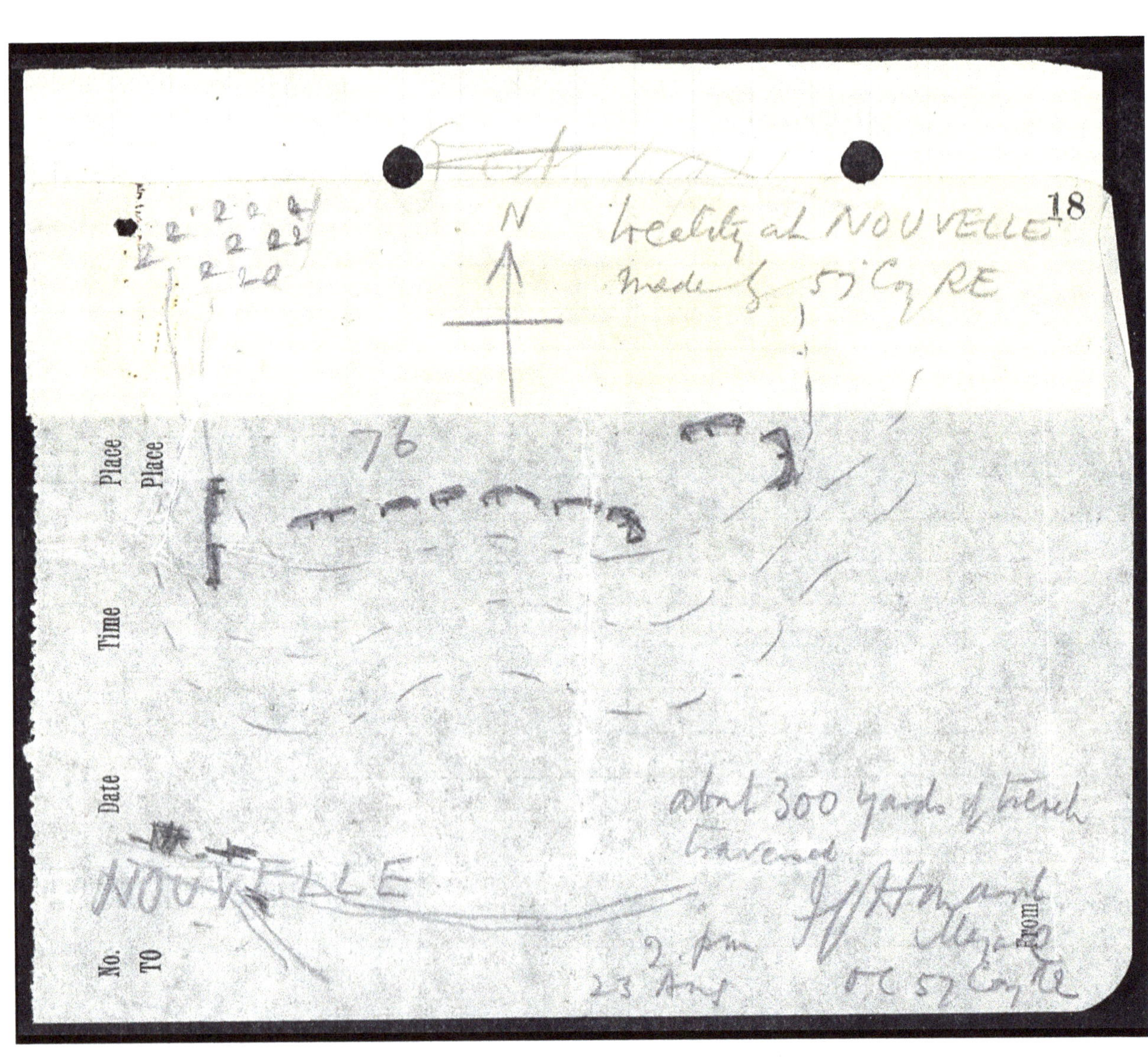
18

N

locality at NOUVELLE made by 57 Coy RE

76

NOUVELLE

about 300 yards of trench traversed

2 pm
23 Aug

JJ Howard
Major
OC 57 Coy RE

No.
TO
Date
Time
Place
Place
From

Sept. 1914

www.ingramcontent.com/pod-product-compliance
Lightning Source LLC
Chambersburg PA
CBHW081450160426
43193CB00013B/2431